MW00936901

Granny's Old Hands

What Has She Been Doing With Them?
Granny's Coming Out of the Closet

by

Celestine Starks

authorHOUSE™

1663 Liberty Drive, Suite 200
Bloomington, Indiana 47403
(800) 839-8640
www.AuthorHouse.com

First published by AuthorHouse 01/18/06

ISBN: 1-4208-8098-5 (sc)

Printed in the United States of America
Bloomington, Indiana

This book is printed on acid-free paper.

Without the support, love and
commitment from my family,
This book would have never been penned.
I thank God
For them and all the opportunities they allowed
Me to raise my old hands to praise Him.

To both my parents who watch me
From their resting place in Heaven,
I am grateful for the foundation
You both provided me with.

To all my sisters and brothers,
I love you dearly.

To Preston, my husband, critic and
friend, your dry sense of humor
Has always been a blessing to me.

To my own dear children, to God be the Glory.
To LaQuan, my grandson, thank
you for your honesty.
To Kinney Dean who taught me the
proper way to drink orange juice
To R.D. and Mary Starks, thank you all

To Aunt Ovia and Aunt Ella who
wanted me when no one else did.
To Nadine and Willie and Doshia, Ray
Margaret and Bernice Raspberry,
To every church mother and granny
who believed in me, I say thank you all.
To my New Jerusalem Church family
and Pastors Charles & Fran Bicy,
MSU/CEDP dreams do come true.
To all of my friends, Ms. Ada, my editor
and office daughter, Alisha Earle,
To all my Daughter of Destiny friends who
provided me the encouragement I needed last
February regarding this work, thank you
Last but not least of all, all my late
night walking buddies, thank you.

I would like to dedicate this small token of
Work to all the grannies across this world.

It doesn't matter the color of your skin,
The size of your hands
Or the wrinkles that show signs of
Wear and tear on your hands

Because you will come to know,
just as I discovered in
My life that I was fearfully and wonderfully
Made in the image and likeness of God.

Many of you reading this small token
Of love may not realize how beautiful
Your hands are as grannies,

But visit with me for a few brief moments and
You will discover just as I did to appreciate and
Assume the position of raising your wrinkled,
Tried and worn hands to Him in praise.

No matter how difficult the trial you faced,
No matter which person(s) was responsible
For your hands being held in
an upward position,
You shall never be the same and neither shall I.

Table of Contents

Preface

Dear Reader,

Just like every writer, producer, actor and director, I wanted something that would grab your attention from the very first line penned. Most of my adult life has been filled with suggestions from friends and family members advising me to sit down and share some of those outstanding events that have occurred in my life.

I had started many times to answer that call, but it wasn't until one of my precious grandchildren got my attention in the most dramatic way. If I have learned anything in life it's that when it comes to dealing with children, they will tell you the truth and nothing but the truth. Children are innocent; therefore, unable to conjure up what we want to hear as adults but what we need to hear.

The day my grandson informed me about the condition regarding my old hands, tears began to roll down my cheeks for a few moments and eventually found a safe resting place underneath much of the excess weight my true self hides behind. I wanted to yell back at him," Well if your hands had been some of the places mine had been or done some of the difficult things I had to do, buddy, yours would look old also." But, I didn't.

I just walked away and from that day to this one, I never forget to question myself about my life each and every time I look at my old hands. I began to examine whether or not it had been really worth it to subject my hands to many of life's ups and downs, which I thought had allowed me to live and walk away a winner as a granny.

That brief conversation with my grandson changed my life fundamentally that day. For me it helped to set in motion for me a new perspective and appreciation for each and every day I live. I began to see the wonder in God's love for me as a granny in marvelous ways. I also saw how God used something as innocent as my grandson's remarks to get me off my rear end and face each day in His presence. I now lift my old hands to praise Him. I praise Him for this opportunity to share with you some of the personal experiences that have happened in my life over a period of time. It may appear that my life had no order but once you finish reading, you will see that it really does.

I skipped around sharing different time periods and brief encounters from incidents that probably could have taken me out of this world or caused me to have a nervous breakdown but as a determined granny with old hands, I wanted you all to know how the power of prayer and a relationship with the Lord Jesus Christ have sustained me and my family. Will you join me as I come out of the closet I created for myself? I am no longer ashamed of the events that took place over the course of my life. I realize that God has always had my entire life in His control. Please join in with me as I laugh, sometimes even crying, for a brief period knowing that with uplifted hands to praise and worship Him, God finds pleasure in me.

I hope you will!

Celeste Starks

Chapter 1

Grandson's Revelation

"Dang Granny, Your Hands are Old!"

Talk about a person forgetting his/her history. This small chap of mine (my grandson) had no knowledge about how I drove for sixteen hours through unfamiliar territory with his uncle, my son, who at the time was only eleven years old, to witness his birth but how could he? The purpose of this all important trip was to provide some extra love and comfort to my daughter who was set to deliver this little blessing. I shall never forget how much courage I had to muster up for this endeavor. I was the only driver for this trip and I was quite fearful, literally. I had budgeted the money out to the last brown penny. Of course, my little soon-to-be born grandson had no idea what I had gone through just to make this trip. He never knew that I had to stop my automobile along interstate I-75 South to catch a nap, only to have the state police inform me of the purposes of the beautiful rest stops located a few more miles down the road. I had always heard the stories about lewd and lascivious behavior occurring along those rest stops, and I must admit that I was afraid of who or what I might encounter. My son was my responsibility and I was not about to put him in a position to see or hear unlawful things that I was not prepared for. The state police changed all that. I couldn't stay along the side of the highway. I had been forced to make a decision and I did. I moved my automobile. The intent was to keep gas in the vehicle and keep moving, moving towards Jacksonville, North Carolina.

Many of my immediate family members thought I had lost what little mind I had left, but a granny will go to the ends of the earth if necessary to witness the arrival of her first grandchild. This was my mission. My grandson couldn't have known how terrified I was each time I approached the mountains in West Virginia. I really didn't have enough driving experience to tackle something of such magnitude, but I did it anyway. Nor could he have known how my heart dropped each time a large semi-truck passed, thinking only about it sliding down the access ramp if and when it lost speed or control. He couldn't have known the feelings of hopelessness I experienced as I questioned the wonders and workings of God and how good the cool breeze felt as it swept in from the mountains as the night approached us. We were too far from home to turn around, and yet not close enough to feel safe. But long before my grandson met me and had his revelation about my hands, they were in a position of surrender—surrendering to God for His guidance and surrendering to God for the comfort of His care and protection.

I didn't have enough money budgeted in for a hotel and keeping in mind what the state police told me earlier, I had to trust in the Almighty God as I pulled into what seemed to be a rest area with my own precious son. He trusted me for his protection and I was trusting God for the both of us. We did arrive safely after almost sixteen hours between sleeping and driving the distance. I remembered that it was the month of March and what a wonderful time of the year to have a new little person in our family; however, that month had also brought so much sadness for my family. Both my parents passed in March. I expected this new birth to bring with it a different joy. I saw this as redemption and God would help me find new hope for what had once been such a bitter time. My son and I spent a week loving on my daughter and waiting for this tiny chap to arrive. We walked, purchased new items for my grandson's room, cleaned my daughter's house, told stories and employed all the old homemade remedies I had ever heard about that could be used to help my daughter through labor.

We spent our money down to just barely enough for gas for the return trip back to Michigan. Absolutely nothing occurred. From the very beginning, my grandson had a plan of his on. I was scheduled to return back to Michigan because I still had a job and my employer probably wouldn't have understood any longer the purpose of my mission. As difficult as the trip started out to be, I often look back over everything my son and I encountered—the long stretch of I- 75 South and the unfamiliar highway signs—and now understand how all these play an important part in a person's life when he or she launchs towards new adventures. You find strength to trust yourself. I found myself hoping against hope that I would arrive in one piece. I hoped that I could protect my son from the uncertain dangers that the highway most assuredly possessed. And oh, the weather with the ominous dark night that ushered in those ungodly empty sounds, sounds that made one appreciate their own backyard, that played psychological mind games on me. The other drivers knew nothing regarding my situation.

It's been said many times that love knows no fear and unconditional love has no boundaries. I had proven that to myself with this trip. My son and I headed back home, my grandson having the last laugh. Even though he didn't arrive during my visit, five wonderful days later he chose to make an appearance on March 21, 1993. From that day to this one, he's been revealing his thoughts and concerns to his granny, sometimes profoundly and sometimes with just everyday talks that cause me to ask God for His guidance so that when I provide the answers to my grandson's questions, he walks away informed. I can truly be thankful for my old hands; old hands that continue to ache in the cold months during Michigan's bitter winter season, old hands that sometimes find it difficult to twist the tops off jelly jars, old hands that worked in the steel mills in Gary, Indiana early in life, old hands that cleaned the toilets in the home of my high school counselor while her children watched the Saturday morning cartoons and yes, my old hands that will continue to thank God for my grandson's revelations.

My life has changed since that conversation with my grandson. I take the time to appreciate those things about myself I had locked away in the secret chambers of my heart and soul, untouchable to those on the outside because I knew all too well how to camouflage my feelings, my desires and the chances I should have taken on myself way before my grandson's revelation. Now, I am out of the closet living and enjoying the small stuff. When I look at my old hands, I am amazed each and every day at the territory I have covered with them and in spite of how they look, I can still say they are my old hands and to God be the glory. I even mustered up the courage to have my nails done for my daughter's wedding, and I now paint my toenails. And I didn't stop there. Ol' sista-girl bought some colorful eye shadow only to have one of my daughters put it own for me. But that's ok because I'm having a blast living with my old hands!

What a wonderful feeling to know that you really can be OK. No matter what you experience as a granny, it's about the choices you make and your perception of how you view yourselves. There are many closet doors I had to shut and there were many I had to open so I could enjoy what was on the other side. Grannies, all things are possible if you believe in God and yourselves. Listen to your grandsons as they pour their hearts out to you in those small conversations and your lives will change.

Chapter 2

Childhood Memories

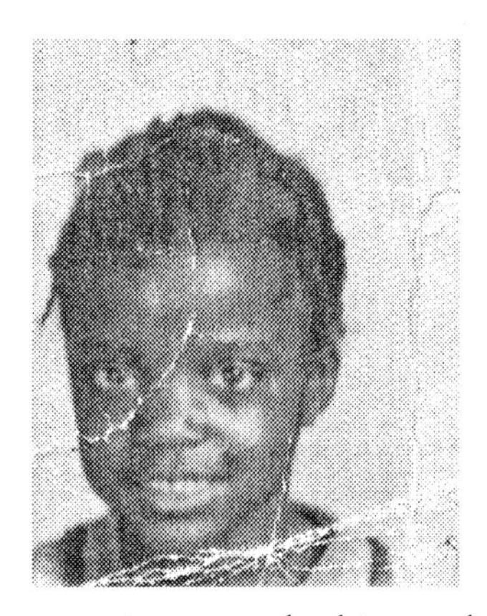

All of my memories are etched in my head and heart; besides I only possess one picture from my childhood that connects me to ever having one.

Chapter 3

No Name on my First Birth Certificate

April 2005

Validation can be an important thing for people who have suffered with many of life's unfortunate experiences and lived to overcome the crushing cruelties of low self-esteem, inferiority and depression. Unbeknownst to the world, I have surreptitiously searched for most of my adult life for someone to validate me. I hid behind smiles, laughter and tears but now as I learn to fight my way out of this bondage, I no longer need outside validation. I am learning to love me and accept the person I am becoming. I believe for these reasons that it's a good time to share a little bit about my personal journey and some of the circumstances of how I entered this life.

Several years ago I got the bright idea to apply for my passport. Why not, I thought. One of my life long dreams had always been to visit other countries. If and when the opportunity arrived, I realized I needed to have valid documentation to travel. In other words, I needed a passport. In the process of gathering the necessary documents needed, I discovered I didn't have a copy of my own birth certificate. I had copies of all my eight siblings' birth certificates but not mine.

I must stop now for a station identification break to inform you how all this transpired... I had the privilege of being born to two wonderful people during the early fifties. Many of us African- American children born during that era really didn't understand a lot of things, but I learned real early that things were different for my family. My dad had served his country during WWII. He possessed many medals, lapel buttons and was issued an honorable discharge from the military for his service. He was a gifted, self-taught auto mechanic. For many years he was employed by one of the largest automobile dealerships in Gary, Indiana. When my dad passed away in March of 1984, he was honored with a flag and a full- fledged military ceremony. He lays to rest peacefully in Battle Creek, Michigan, at Fort Custard. My mom was a high school graduate with a passion for higher education. She had the ability to engage us children in conversations about the world and opportunities that we could benefit from if we stayed focused and paid attention in school. My mom's talent was in sharing stories that fascinated us about people, places and the world in general. We spent many hours in our public library enjoying books, books and more books.

With that said, how then does a person from a two-parent home have a birth certificate with no name on it? Like most African American families during those times, jobs were difficult to secure. The Civil Rights Act of 1957 was introduced in Eisenhower's presidency and it was the act that kick-started the civil rights legislative and program that eventually led to the 1964 Civil Rights Act and the 1965 Voting Rights Act. Many changes had begun to occur in my family during this particular time. My dad was unable to obtain decent work and he was forced to leave the home because "the system" wouldn't allow him to remain. In order for my mom to qualify and get the free government cheese, flour, canned meat, that good old powered milk and the few dollars allowed her from the welfare system, my dad had no other choice but to leave. My mom, with nine children, had to survive with welfare being the only source of income until my dad could find another job and return. I can vividly remember thinking back then why all the trips to the library and why have a daddy in the home one month and then the next month he's gone?

During some of those difficult times, my mom discovered a white pastor in our neighborhood whose church had a clothing surplus store. He would allow her entrance into his church from time to time to pick out clothes for us. Also, the owner of a small corner store allowed her a line of credit to charge food when we ran low just before the government surplus would arrive. So perceptive we are as children that I knew in all this, my mom never totally blamed my dad. She loved him and knew his sufferings were much deeper than most of her immediate family could ever know or understand. My dad did get another job and was allowed back into the home. My mom had to report to the welfare system that my dad had another job but by that time, we were labeled welfare kids and all the stigmas associated with that followed us well into our adult lives.

In the early sixties, my mom's physical body began to deteriorate from the toil and stress life had handed her. Tuberculosis, ulcers, living with the ills of poverty, social injustices and a society that judge her based on the color of her skin helped speed up the process that indelibly changed our lives. My dad had begun to drink to ease the battles he fought and there we were, nine chil dren, wondering from day to day about our own fate. My mom was removed from our home in the early part of 1965. She was placed in a tuberculosis center located in Crown Point, Indiana, for treatment. My dad's drinking took a dramatic turn during that period. The neighbors began to watch his comings and goings. The State of Indiana stepped in and provided us with an aide during the day to see us off to school and take care of us until my dad returned home in the evening. It looked like we were going to make it, but most of you know the history of what can happen to a family when the mom isn't present. You hear about it, but I personally know the destructiveness associated with alcoholism—another book, another chapter.

But briefly, the State of Indiana decided they had done enough to help my dad. They exercised the power of their authority and made the decision to remove all nine of us on October 7, 1965, and I was a ward of the State at the age of 15. We were placed in foster homes, separated by age and gender. I can remember to this day feeling so helpless, mad at my dad for his drinking and my mom for being sick. I knew if she could have just come home all of this would not be happening. I thought about running away and abandoning my sisters and brothers. I wished my mom hadn't had so many children; I blamed them all for invading my life and my time with my mom. I had not had the chance to have my own bedroom nor experience having new clothes that were not hand-me-downs from my older sister. How I hated those black and white oxford shoes of hers I had to wear! I was never going to know what it felt like to be special. In my 15 year old mind, these actions started the progression of my mom's early death at the age of forty-one. Vicariously, I felt the shame, humiliation and the helplessness she must have felt after the State interceded and placed her children in foster homes. This was more than she could bear. My mom died in March of 1966, leaving her nine children unshielded from the cruelties of life and many of the pains associated with having our own scarlet letter—that deep ebony hue of God's love that was more often than not the ridicule of white America and even more regrettably, my own people. We all possessed this mark.

Now years later, and guess what? I discovered the birth certificate that I applied for so I could travel and witness firsthand all those places my mom had shared with me as a child had no name on it. It simply had these words printed in solid, black ubiquitous letters: "INFANT BABY GREER GIRL." What a shock to look down on a piece of paper and realize my name wasn't even important enough to be placed on it! Now, how was I supposed to get my passport and who was going to let my bald, black self into their country without proof of identification? I wondered if my past had come full circle. Was I being punished once again for dreaming about me and making plans to venture outside the boundaries I had lived in for such a long time, or was this just another one of those injustices I had to learn to live with? Well, it took some intervention and work but something wonderful happened to me just a few days before my 55th birthday. One of my sisters surprised me and I am happy to say that at age 55 I now have a birth certificate with my full name on it, Celestine Greer, the year I was born and the State of Indiana's seal on it. I am on my way now, baby! My old hands are lift-ed up praising God for another great opportunity to witness His love on my behalf.

To this day, I still don't know why my name was never on my birth certificate, but that's water under the bridge now. My past has taught me to push forward regardless of the government cheese and the social stigmas attached to my family and me. It's the past and I can use it as a stepping stone to climb to new adventures, or I can continue to hide in the closet of sadness and shame and continually living as a 15 year-old seeking validation from others who have no clue of my worth. Grannies across this great world we live in, lift up your own hands. Lift them high and touch the sky. Lift them higher than high and do more than just enough to get by. It's your time to shine. Come on out of those closets. Lift your old hands like mine are right now. Not later and not in the sweet old bye and bye but now, grannies.

Chapter 4

The Lights Really Do Go Out!

My Knee Baby

My mom was a wonderful human being who had a way with words when she needed to get a point across to her children. She always told us not to say what we would and wouldn't do in this life. Sometimes, she would say that things happen and that we would find ourselves doing some unexpected things where our character and integrity would be tested. She informed us that once we became adults and had our own children, much like she had done so many times for us, sacrifices would be made and our love for our own children would be tested. Well into my adult life I can say my mom was right. There were some things I experienced as a child living with my mom that I swore I would never do, including but not limited to eating government cheese, oatmeal, powered eggs, spam and that potted meat mixed with that dark, overcooked brown gravy. I swore never again to sleep in a house whose running water, heat or lights that had been shut off. Well, guess what? Several years ago I lied and at 53 I heard my mom's voice loud and clear. It took a long time for it to happen but it did. Since my mom's advice many years ago, I've slept on floors, chairs, back seats of small automobiles, cold buses, airplanes, trains and beds with no mattresses. I even slept with my three sisters in the same bed.

What I am about to share with you is the truth, the whole truth so help me God. I have already closed the door of shame that tried so hard to destroy my life early on so please don't feel sorry for what I am about to share. I call it taking advantage of another opportunity to see my survival skills in action. I have been fortunate enough to birth three wonderful children of my own and I also have two-step children. All of them have been on my heart as infants and now into their adulthoods I have what I call a knee baby. When I was a child, the old people down South used to say that your children are on your heart when they are small, but when they become adults you will find yourself on your knees praying to God on their behalves. Now, for the lack of better terminology, I really do have a knee baby. I know I've spent many hours on my knees where she is concerned, not for behavioral problems but for the sickness that invaded her frail body each and every time she was about to reach some major goal in her life. I have practiced tough love with her, emotional love, sound love, foolish love and this journey

I am about to share with you encompasses unconditional love in its highest form where a parent and a child are concerned.

In 2002, I literally went up and down Interstate 55 South eight times to Memphis, Tennessee, visiting my hospitalized child. I traveled by car when time allowed, flew on airplanes when money was available and I spent many a trip on the good old Greyhound bus. I remember the last time I had to go. My daughter had already been admitted to the hospital when I received the call. I decided this was to be the last time I would go. My grandchildren would have to return back with me and when my daughter was strong enough, I would return to move her back home. My husband was working the second shift at his job and he was well aware of what had transpired. He knew how worn and tried my physical body had become, and he watched and heard my cries as I had to come to terms with another eighteen-hour bus ride. I had no choice but to leave my job that day earlier than usual.

I packed a few items and left Lansing, Michigan. I boarded the 7:25 pm bus with a foot long submarine sandwich and a large white 16 ounce Styrofoam cup of ice that were held captive in a plastic bag. These two items were to last me the duration of the trip. The sandwich had been cut into fourths and at each major stop I replenished the cup with ice. My nephew was kind enough to drop me off and provide this meal for me. I had to change buses in Chicago, which is always a treat. I believe people come from all over the world just to change buses there—single mothers and fathers, young and old. The line for Memphis is always long no matter how early you arrive. You see bags tied with ropes and belts, plastic bags containing food and people hoping for the best as they make their connections.

I made eye contact and smiled at a few people in line. I thought it important for them to know what I looked like in case something happened on the bus. September 11 did change our world, but the love of a mother with a child in trouble supercedes any fears that attempt to invade her consciousnesses. It's like I switched gears and during that time of trouble, the love I had for my child sustained me. Even though those other people in line couldn't image what I was experiencing, at least I thought someone would remember I smiled. It never ceases to amaze me that while standing in those long lines how often I wondered about stories they could share with me about themselves while they stood in those long lines. I wondered what pain they had carried around. Were some of them enroute to rescue a loved one or were they headed for a new life? The food court is expensive in Chicago! I was able to have a person watch my belongings while I got another Styrofoam cup filled with ice. Once permitted to board the bus, I managed to get the back seat. It made for a nice place to stretch my tried body and prepare for the long ride.

I had received word before leaving Lansing that my daughter was able to have a young girl baby-sit for my grandchildren prior to my arrival, and that she would have to leave in order to get ready for school the next morning. I am eighteen hours away and frustrated but determined to make the best of the trip once again. My grandchildren had to be placed with another person, as she also had to get ready for school the next morning. I arrived in Memphis the next morning around 11:00 am and was met by one of my daughter's friends who had been kind enough to get the children off to school.

I went straight to the hospital, washed my face in my daughter's room and introduced myself to the nursing staff. I made sure they knew I was in from out of town. I didn't want them thinking no one cared about my daughter. She had spent some crucial hours there without any family members. They needed to know she was loved and cared for. I spoke with her doctors only to be informed of the paralysis the stroke had caused and other conditions that had invaded her small, frail body. By mid-afternoon, I had already picked up my daughter's automobile from the hospital parking lot where she left it upon her arrival. I had learned how to get back and forth to the hospital so I picked my grandchildren up from school, met the principal and their teachers and headed back to the hospital for a third time that day.

I managed to get us all back to my daughter's apartment safely, passing the Krispy Kream donut shop located on Elvis Presley Boulevard along the way. What a treat to actually drive down these famous street hours after standing in line in Chicago at the Greyhound bus station. Isn't life one big barrel of laughs? Everyone had his or her bath, and I was really feeling like I had accomplished something good that night. Prayers were said, the grands spoke with their mom briefly on the phone and off to bed we all went.

The next day for me arrived a somewhat earlier than I was used to but so what, I am a granny with old hands and ready to successfully meet the goals for the day: 1) drop the kids off at school 2) pick them up from school 3) visit the hospital 4) do homework and 5) speak with the doctors. My daughter's gallbladder would have to be removed in the next couple of days because her blood pressure indicated she would have another stroke. I don't know to this day how the stroke and gallbladder are related, but they did remove it on the second day of my visit. The third day arrived as did the bight brilliance of the sun in the sky. It hanged around just long enough for me to enjoy the beauty of God and His creation. It was the same routine except we had treats on the way home. Can you guess where we stopped? Krispy Kream, of course.

Once again I must relate that this is in fact a true account of nine days spent on a journey reevaluating my love for my knee baby who lay in the hospital at the mercy of God, doctors, nurses and many laboratory technicians. The next day did arrive but with it came a trial that would change my life once again. I had dropped the older two children off at school and the baby and I stayed back at the apartment. We were singing along with Barney on TV and had just finished saying our morning prayers, agreeing that Barney could fill in while we prepared to go back to the hospital, when a silence fell upon the house. The sound was interrupted on the TV. My first thought was that the signal had been lost but not so. The silence I was experiencing was the electricity being shut off. I managed to get to the back door just in time to see the person from the local Memphis Light & Gas and Water Company disconnecting my daughter's services. I quickly tried to explain what was going on in my daughter's life and that I was just visiting to help out. I even opened the door wide enough so she could see that my small grandchild lived here. I was informed of what it would cost to have the services restored and was even provided the necessary phone numbers to call for assistance. I was given five days to take care of this bill or the other services would be interrupted. I thanked the lady and returned to the living room. I literally dropped to my knees and as God as my witness, I lifted my arms up and began to sing. My precious grandchild did the same thing. While I was on my knees, I discovered I could still function in the midst of this heavy trial. I had just enough money available to rent a U-haul truck to relocate my daughter's belongings and my grandchildren back to Lansing. I phoned my husband and informed him of what had taken place. He provided the best advice he could considering the fact he knew my finances and what I was working with. I dressed my grandchild and myself and decided the best thing I could do was make a trip to one of the local discount stores I had seen on the way to the hospital. I purchased some battery operated lights, a small 5 inch TV and a radio. I picked the other children up from school and in formed them we would be playing an adventurous game when they got home. We went to the hospital, visited my daughter and left just before the streetlights caught us.

Things were going well until the fifth day. Memphis Light & Gas and Water did return this time to shut off the water and the gas. I packed a small bag before picking the children up from school and contacted the nursing staff, expressing a desire to spend extra time with my daughter in her room. Since I had come so far, it wasn't inconceivable that I wanted to spend more one-on-one time with her. They allowed it. There was a small cot placed in my daughter's room for the children and I slept on two chairs put together. Thank God she was in a single room. I kept the children outside as long as the night permitted so they could play with their friends before returning back to the hospital. I was so terrified the neighbors would discover the plight of my situation and report me to the children's protection service. I panicked so many times. I was an adult on a mission and the good I was attempting to do could have caused me my grandchildren. No greater love does a granny have for her daughter and grandchildren than to sacrifice herself!

My grandchildren and I showered in my daughter's hospital room. I dressed them early enough to be dropped off at school and while the weather allowed, I would go to the apartment and pack my daughter's belongings by the modest daylight I had on my side. This went on for six days. I still praised God and I lifted my hands to worship Him, as did my grandchildren. On the eighth day, one of my sisters arrived to help me pack my daughter's belongings. When she discovered our situation and how we were basically living in the hospital room, she rented a hotel room and we spent the night. We repeated the same pattern of visiting my daughter during the day and packing the U-Haul truck I had rented in the evening. I managed to get my hands on the necessary documents I needed to enroll my grandchildren in school once we arrived back in Lansing.

We all spent Thanksgiving Day 2002 with my daughter in the hospital. I left her automobile in the parking lot of the hospital and traveled the next sixteen hours with a packed U-Haul truck, fearful and unsure of the obstacles I would face with three grandchildren and my sister following in her vehicle. We arrived in Lansing Thanksgiving night around 11:58 pm, just in time to enjoy the meal my husband had prepared for us. I raised my hands, my old hands to thank God for his protection over the highway and for His wisdom and courage that He provided me in my decision to stay in my daughter's apartment without any utilities. I raised my hands for the guidance He offered and the will He supplied me in not succumbing to the fears that tried to invade and conquer my soul. I raised my old hands in worship to God for I knew there were grannies all over the world that had experienced much worse than I had. Please share with others how your God has kept you safe in these trying times. Once again, to God be the glory, for this granny with old hands will continue to use them for the glory and honor of having the opportunity to be connected with my Heavenly Father. He created me in his image and likeness and allowed me to experience this journey with my knee baby.

Chapter 5

The Waiting Room

All Eyes on Me

God created us with the ability to use our fives senses. We have the capacity to smell, touch, hear, see and taste. There are some smells that I shall never forget. The smell in hospitals is one that I have an acute awareness of. When my daughter was hospitalized out of state, I became attentive to those long corridors, the patterns and shapes on the walls, the different colored uniforms the staff wore and the floors where patients in critical condition were kept. I learned some of the codes that were sounded over the intercom systems. I knew when different families were being summoned to meet the doctors in those miniature rooms located in quite places so they could exchange words regarding their love ones.

Now on this particular day, I faced the raw realities of life and some of those smells that once held me captive. I lifted my old hands up to evoke the mercies of God to sustain everything in me. God would prove to me that I was created in His image; therefore, I could call on Him and He would answer. It was time for me to do my part also. The real "I" in Christ needed to show up. No mask, no pretending, just show up and take care of the business at hand. Once again, life had dealt my family a blow that could change the structure of our entire lives.

When you get a call from the hospital letting you know that your child is in trouble, what happens then? Picture the sheer panic and what-ifs that are flowing so freely through your insides and at any moment you can break, yet you don't because you know everyone is looking at you to hold everything together. And with all those external and internal struggles you have going on, why do they put you in that small five by five room where you and everybody else waiting know you're about to receive a bad report from someone on the medical staff?

I responded to the call from the hospital only to be stopped by hospital security. When I approached my child's room, I could hear these audible yet whimpering like sounds coming from her. They almost sounded inhuman as if she were fighting between this world and the next one to hold on. I collected my thoughts and pulled myself together. Just hours ago, I had spoken with the nurse and she informed me all was well. My child was resting peacefully and she relayed that if there were any changes the hospital staff would call. I continued to plan my mid-morning schedule at work and I made sure the nurse had my work and cell numbers. In fact, I was thinking about my own doctor's appointment later that afternoon.

Now standing outside the intensive care room where doctors, nurses, technicians and hospital nursing supervisors are looking on as my child is administered CPR, my mind drifts and I'm reflecting on everything up to this point. I'm told someone will talk to me shortly. When someone does arrive, I'm informed that my child's heart has stopped once and for now they need me to wait in a closet-like room down the hall. They assure me someone will come speak to me momentarily.

The hospital security person directed me to the waiting room down the hall. He was called in just in case I decided to cut up and act a fool. Other family members began arriving. The hospital chaplain was there and the ministers from my own church arrived. I made small talk with family members and for a few moments, I had them laughing about something that occurred a few days earlier. They couldn't possibly know my own heart was about to burst. I appeared to have it all together, for you see, it was my knee baby who was in trouble once again. My mind returned to her three children. Just eight days ago, I had arrived back home to Lansing with a U-haul truck packed with all their belongings, shifting and rearranging my household to accommodate her belongings. What would I tell them this time? They knew the routine. Each time their mother went to the hospital, granny had been there. Whether it was three days or three weeks, granny found her way there. Their mother had survived a stroke and gall bladder removal just a month ago while in Memphis and now less than eight days later and in a different state, she was back in the hospital fighting once again in a battle for her life.

It had been almost an hour and finally someone from the nursing administrative staff came in to talk to my family and me. She was pleasant and her voice was calm, but I'm a mom and I could see trouble on her face. I knew the look and I felt the pain as she prepared to share with me what had taken place in the last few hours. I approached her as a mom and asked her for the truth. Her response was not good as she was describing to me and all those in the waiting room what had just happened. Once again, my child's heart had stopped, and now my family and I were faced with the realities of what might occur in the next few hours. All eyes were on me and the support of my husband, my other children and friends and family surrounded me. News travels fast, sometimes faster than the time needed to process what actions are warranted in circumstances such as these. Now, my own mind was racing with thoughts from conversations my child and I had just before dawn and her arrival at the hospital. Did I say I loved her, or did I remind her of how tried I was of changing and rearranging my life for her and my grandchildren?

I had spent bill money that I needed to help her, bought automobiles for her, purchased stoves for her that were then left in newly rented houses once she decided she needed to relocate to a different state, and wired money in the middle of the night. You name it, I had done it. I had sent packages through the mail for birthdays and Christmas and had bought clothes for the grandchildren over and over again. I had just gotten my home back in order from the last time my daughter decided to come home for a visit that lasted almost two years. Finally, I could enjoy having a spare room in our home just for myself with all the things in it I never had as a child—stuffed animals lined across the bed, my own TV, CD player and a floral arrangement of some of the finest flowers you ever saw. Now once again, sacrifices would have to be made. My grand- children would have to be enrolled in school and day care facilities and transportation would have to be arranged around my work schedule. I couldn't and didn't dare share these thoughts with anyone else in the room. How cruel and selfish they would think I was being. Yet as I sat in that claustrophobic room boxed in with all those people, I knew I needed to show them my strength. I couldn't and didn't dare break down. I wanted to scream from deep inside my belly that I had had enough! Why didn't she listen to me eight years ago when I warned her about the premature marriage she was about to enter into? She was just a baby but no, it had to be her way and now here I sit in this cramped room dealing with emotions I dared not share. After the nurse left, it seemed like two hours passed before the doctor came in the room. We all watched his facial expressions and we knew the news was even more devastating.

Yet again, the news was heart breaking. My child's heart had stopped two more times, and they were prepared for the worst. The doctor suggested we call in any relatives and support we needed. They were going to clean up the mess in the room where she was and then my husband and I were allowed to see her. I thanked the doctor and proceeded to have my other children make phone calls to family members. All eyes were still on me. I got up from that seat and excused my self. There are always small bathrooms located next to these rooms they put you in; I needed to have a conversation all by myself where no one was watching and listening to what I was about to say. I proceeded to the bathroom, opened the door and looked in the mirror located directly in front of me. Once I closed the door, I looked straight in that mirror and for the first time since my initial phone call to check on my daughter, I could see my face. No make up on, nothing to hide behind. It was just me looking directly in the mirror. I lifted my old hands up as I had done in Memphis just a few days earlier. My request was a simple one. I didn't ask God and I didn't beg God for me. I only requested that He would let my daughter know that I was there in the room with her, and if she wanted to fight to stay alive then that would become my fight as well. I never cried one tear; I only asked that she be aware of my being and presence.

I washed my face with the coarse, white towel paper and found my way back to the waiting room. The medical staff had come to take my husband and me down that long, cold corridor to the room where my daughter's life was suspended in time. I saw monitors, cords, machines, and a frail ninety-eight pound person lying so very still and connected to a breathing machine and heart monitor. I could actually hear my own heart pounding in my chest. I could taste the medicines they had used on her. I could feel the cold sting of death lurking in the room, and I could see the results of the constant pounding on my daughter's chest after CPR was administered. I stood on the left side of the bed. My husband stood on the other. I bent down to her ear level and repeated those same words I had echoed in the bathroom a few moments ago. I said her name softly in her ear and whispered to her, "If you want to stay here, I'll fight with you." That's all I said. Naturally, she was not able to respond but a mother knows and for the next five days my child laid unaware of her surroundings, deep in a sleep that only God could bring her out of.

Five days later and many opportunities to lift my old hands up to Him in praises, my daughter woke up about 4:00 am. For the next forty-nine days, three different pacemaker/difibulator combinations were installed and tried in my daughter. We walked the corridors of that hospital praising God once again with uplifted hands for another miracle. During those most crucial days, grannies, I found out that you do have a choice to either give in or be honest with yourselves. You have the ability to position yourselves to stay in the fight. I realized that some fights may not have a happy ending, as this one did for my family, but I learned without a shadow of a doubt that God will sustain you when the battle appears too much for you. He will step in and remind you of how those waiting room experiences can change your life. He will even take pleasure in an old granny raising her hands in praise to worship Him for allowing her to pour her heart out in honesty about her fears, struggles and sometimes the overwhelming burdens we have to bear. God never leaves us; He just picks us up and carries us so that our hands are free to raise up to Him in praise.

I hope and pray your waiting room experiences will draw you closer to God as all eyes will be on you as grannies, mothers, sisters, fathers, brothers, aunts and uncles in your time of difficulties. I hope you find strength to come out of your closets after having spoken to God about your experiences. You will see how the love of God can sustain you. Lift your old hands up, knowing all things are possible for those who believe. My daughter has been out of the hospital for almost a full year. The last time she was admitted, I was admitted also. I had exhausted my body. I spent five days down the hall from her. I had to come out of another closet only to realize I was not supermom. I was just a mother and granny who had pushed too far and too long. We are grateful that for the first time since this journey, my daughter has not missed her children's birthdays or spending time with them for the holidays. She still fights to stay alive and every now and then I whisper in her ear that I will fight to keep her here if that's what she desires, but she must also lift her hands to praise and worship God for His goodness in your life. Grannies, I wouldn't trade my old hands for anything this world could offer.

I hope by now after joining in this journey with me you will appreciate your old hands. Come out, come on out. You will be surprised at all those doors you can shut and the people you will bless by sharing your journey. Come out of your closets.

Chapter 6

Granny Gotta Represent: Yeah, Right!

The Gas Station

Imagine being a 54 year-old granny driving around town in a shinny, big black Expedition. I need a small step stool to climb in, and I definitely have to catch my breath once I place my large buttocks in the front seat of that big old hunk of iron and steel. I know the conditions of my bad knees. The doctors say it's arthritis mixed with a worn out body, but I climb in anyway. Other drivers see me and they smile. From time to time, I'm stopped at the light side-by- side with another Expedition with people in it the same ages as my son, Michael. The music is blasting really loud from their vehicle. I don't see them at first but the woofer speakers are blaring, and then I notice heads bobbing and my heart racing from the speakers they've installed. They have those du rags on their head.

Every now and then, I bob my head also. I want to appear really cool in my husband's Expedition so I give a little play as I hope the young men are watching me. I wonder if I should raise my window or raise my old hands. I can only image what they may be thinking, but who cares because for a few moments, I know I'm the flavor of the month. I can now see the young man in the passenger's side lean forward and peek inside the window of my vehicle. I'm sure he sees the gray hairs standing at attention on my head. I don't care about that either. All they can possibly think is that this granny has got it going on. What they really don't see us how tight I am gripping the steering wheel, hoping the light will hurry up and change. My mind drifts to replay the events of the day. So much left undone and bills to pay and deadlines to meet at work.

Where does the time go? I had a plan when I was younger—obey my parents, come home early from dates, get good grades in school and grow up and try to make a difference in the world. I can only faintly hear the music because inside my vehicle, I have another conversation going on with myself about the events of my day. I know how the best made plans can change in the blink of an eye. Little did I know back then that something called life could rearrange and change all my plans? I always had conversations about how things would turn out for me, but how naïve I was. Sometimes life just happens and you deal with it between stops at a traffic light or in the doctor's office after receiving bad news about your health, or after receiving a notice informing you the dealership would like to have their automobile back if you don't make a payment as soon as possible. The noise from outside grows more faint. I can hear my own sounds now more clearly, more concisely. Just what are you doing with your old hands, granny? Where will you take them today?

I am a college graduate with three Bachelor of Arts Degrees and a dual Masters Degree. I never smoked nor drank alcoholic beverages. I've slept with only two men, both of whom I married. And now I sit here at the light trying to be cool. It appears that my whole life is at a stand still. Instantly, I am brought back to the present situation because I hear a faint beeping sound. It isn't the music from the neighbor's Expedition; it's my gas light warning signal reminding me it is time to refuel. Now, I really have to face the music. I'm days away from payday and this large, black vehicle is about to embarrass me in the worst way by running out of gas on a major street while I am sitting at the traffic light. There is no music playing now. I tune out all the noise from outside as well as my own internal noise. I pray for a miracle to make it to the nearest gas station. Just in the nick of time, the light changes and I find the courage to make the right turn and head for the nearest gas station. I have never pushed myself in this vehicle to the point where the gaslight came on. I drive a very small automobile and I know exactly where and when enough is enough when it comes to the gas gauge.

I continue my conversation with myself about what just occurred. Why is it so important for me to appear cool, and who gives life permission to just show up when it isn't convenient? I make it to the gas station only to continue my drama. I discover that I, at age fifty-four years- old and driving this big, shinny Expedition trying to impress some young buck, only have twelve shinny quarters that come to exactly $2.50. How can I even think about going into the store and paying the attendant with such a small amount? I have no choice. Once more, I have to play this role of being cool.

I wait until the last person comes out of the station and I proceed to go in and lay my quarters on the attendant's counter. I ask for the requested amount. As I exit the station, out of nowhere the gas bays begin to fill up with other automobiles. In a million years, I bet you this station would never have serviced this amount of customers this time of day. But here I stand with the nozzle in my hand pumping $2.50 worth of gas, refusing or should I say choosing not to remove the nozzle when it reached the amount I paid for. But oh no, I keep the nozzle in my tank, giving the other customers the impression that I am filling up the truck. I raise my free hand and I give the biggest wave I can to the other customers as they look at me. I'm sure the attendant is confused. He knows the pump has stopped and he has to know that I know I should move on, but I don't. Here I am once again, like I was at the light, trying to impress other people.

They surely cannot know I am here with this Expedition only able to pump $2.50 worth of gas. Who cares and so what, I'm thinking to myself but I am enjoying this. I'm a 54 year-old and this granny gotta represent! Yeah, right! I must have stood there forever waving my free hand, smiling and holding the nozzle, all the while making the biggest fool of myself again. It shouldn't matter and just like the immature behavior I exhibited at the light, I had succumb once again at the gas station. I wanted to be cool and I misused an opportunity to extol God by raising my hand artifical praise instead of true praise. Sometimes, grannies can be foolish with their old hands. I finally remove the nozzle.

I am not sure the attendant ever understood what happened nor did the person waiting in line behind me because I'm pretty positive he was wondering why it took so long to pump $2.50 worth of gas. Rest assured, life itself will continue to provide opportunities that challenge us. We don't need to but know this, it becomes dangerous when we seek approval from things, our positions, status or people. I make certain when I drive that big truck I have gas and money. I make sure when I raise my old hands it's unquestionable now that it's only to give God the praise that's due Him. Grannies, we don't have to show ourselves off; God will as we live for him. He will lift us up like a light that sits on a dark hill so the world may see the pleasure he takes in us. We can have fun but we shouldn't waste the time God has allowed us for His business. What a difficult closet to come out of. Granny has to find a better way to represent. Yeah, right!

Chapter 7

Wrinkled and Worn

The Truth Does Hurt

We live in an age where the world is continually changing. We have access to the best technology available. We can beam in conversations through distance learning technology, an individual can actually remain in the comfort of home and complete a college degree program, and we also have the ability to transform an entire classroom into a virtual learning center where students have the capacity to interact with other students from across the world. We call this the age of information and technology. I had the opportunity to broaden my educational experience by returning to school later in my adult life. I was hungry to close the gap between what I thought I knew and what this new learning journey would expose me to. I was so far behind the times. It had been over twenty years since I attended any type of school, so I was really stuck somewhere between the new math and the rich history of African-Americans that was only now slowly filtering through the educational systems. I was reading and having conversations about people from different parts of the world. These people had made significant contributions to the world, and I never knew some of them existed. I was on a roll. Access to information and technology were changing things for me and I was ready to explode.

I always had a passion for African American history. I thought God had created me to help change our world and the views regarding equality and justice for persons with my same skin tone. I can remember engaging in deep discussions with one of my undergraduate professors that somehow always ended up on Africa. He discovered his true self while on a mission there with the Peace Corps one summer.

I developed a hunger for this hidden treasure not realizing that one day it would help me change the direction my life had been going in. I must reinforce how powerful technology, knowledge and information are. These three powerful sources provided the platform I needed to deal with some painful truths regarding the freedom I had been searching for. There were some more closets I had been held captive in, and I wanted out.

We must never forget to pass these three sources on and remind our children's children about them and the power they represent. The beauty of this truth can change our world if instructed on how to use it correctly. You really can be free even if you're locked up physically, emotionally or spiritually like I had been for so many years.

For that reason it's vitally important that we continue to look for ways to close these gaps between those who have access to knowledge and information and those who don't. I knew the truth and had the information. I realized others could be hurt or disappointed in me if I shared what had been shut up in my closet, surrounded by a brick wall. I can actually confess that at one period of my life with all this information and knowledge, I never considered myself special, unique or even wonderful until much later. When I think of all the missed opportunities I let slip away because I had such low self worth I can really kick myself. We often hear how hindsight is so much clearer and retrospective after the fact. I would sure like to have a daily dose of hindsight before things happen.

I shared with you how I arrived on this planet. You already know I was small in weight size at birth. I arrived 2 pounds and 15 ounces. I survived during the fifties when neonatal care was basically nonexistent and was nowhere near the modern technological advancements we have today. What a blessing for me to have survived. I enjoyed the pleasures of having nappy hair as a small child for the most part of my life.

However, I carried all the weight and judgments associated with being labeled a little, old black child. I will speak more on that subject later. This particular journey that I am about to share with you hit me dead smack in the center core of my heart. I did not fathom the future holding any bright dreams for me, nor could I look down the road of life and see some cheerleader coaxing me on to continue this journey. It forced me to deal with the turbulence that occurred in my life at an early age. Turbulence is such a destructive thing if not calmed. The North American English Dictionary defines turbulence as a state of confusion characterized by unpredictability and uncontrolled change, profound uncertainty.

The turmoil that occurred in my childhood prompted me to open this closet door. Once you open up a door you either have to deal with what's on the other side or you discover ways to keep what you saw suppressed deep, deep inside. I chose to walk right in and take the closet doors off the hinges once and for all.

I have already articulated how much I loved my parents and how my family was hit with life altering trials one after the other. What I haven't shared was what prompted me to think so little of myself; consequently, rendering me helpless when this second wave of turbulence showed up. There was no hiding place big enough for me. Changes had begun to occur and the winds had shifted in my life once again. The judicial system, with greater power and authority than I had, used their influence to change the course and direction of my life when I was placed in foster care. I was in an unpredictable, unstable environment with little or no control over it. Early in my adolescent life, this instability helped to buttress a wall that I erected around myself; a self-made brick wall. I built it turbulent brick by turbulent brick with self-hate, doubt and shame as the foundation.

Each brick came to represent some tragic incident that was brought on by a new wave of overpowering turmoil in my life. I was unsafe and untouchable to those around me. I had used the best cement available to construct the bricks used for the wall. I didn't allow air or water to seep in. I didn't even allow myself to take a breath. I wasn't living; I just existed. I had learned the necessary skills needed to go through the motions required for living in this world, but I was not connected to it. I made no noise concerning who I was. As a result, no one ever questioned my identity nor did they ask for my credentials. I had a social security card, my library card, and a plastic card verifying I was a member of the Columbia House Record Club. I never caused any employer I worked for trouble. I went to work on time. I didn't drink nor smoke or introduce any harmful substances into my body. I couldn't even dance. People, as well as some of my family members, just allowed me to go through life without ever questioning the purpose of the wall I had erected.

This wall I built allowed me to hide my hands and hang my head in shame because of things that had occurred in my life. I had experienced failure and disappointments early in life. I knew people's word meant nothing anymore and I also knew love came with a non-refundable price tag. I enjoyed the wall I built. I had control of how the rest of my life would be played out. I had used my old hands to do many things while hiding behind my wall in my own private closet. I can remember throwing them up just as a knife was being hurdled at my throat, or the time a broom was used to chock me as I tried to protect my mother from my drunken dad's attack. My wall protected me from the shame I felt from having such a large frame for a female.

My hands are extremely large, resembling the pictures of my ancestors who picked cotton in the deep, hot South or maybe the ones from the Homeland who commanded great armies. I have always struggled with my appearance. At one time, the color of my skin held me hostage. It's a smooth, deep, and chocolate black with a glistening glow and dimples imbedded in both cheeks. I thought I was indeed cursed by God Almighty but as said in most Sunday morning black folks' church services, "God didn't make junk." So, I had to develop an appreciation for the color of my skin. It's truly a blessing. This has been a painful closet to come out of but necessary if I was ever going to be free from the past that followed me for the better part of my adult life. I had a wall to knock down before I could come out of the closet.

I watched from a front row seat the deterioration of my life. It unfolded piece-by-piece, sometimes in color and at times it even showed up in black and white. I learned to hide behind laughter and sadness when it was convenient. I was always the one to tell the joke about myself before anybody else could. I became obsessed with being a good student in school. I was a good girl, a church worker and a big sister, a clean housewife and a diligent mother, a doormat, a good friend, a bus driver for the local church I fellowshipped at and most of all, a fool for many to misuse at my expense. Disorder had forced me to raise my hands for protection against one of life's cruelest invasions that a child can be subjected to—sexual abuse at the hands of two different relatives who were also hiding behind their own closet doors because of the malicious things they had encountered in their own lives. Unfortunately, I became one of their victims and the outlet for all of their rage, self-loathing and anger that was buried deep within from their childhoods. The mighty winds erupted from this new violent storm in my life, causing a gusty, unpredictable flow of events from another human being who felt it okay to violate my personal temple. They were using their hands for something dirty and unnatural while I was trying to use mine to wash away the shame and guilt that were left. Their actions had added more bricks to my wall and these new bricks became the catalyst for me to hate my very existence. I looked for more bricks to build a more solid wall to cover and protect me.

Then one day I discovered with all my knowledge and information that the wall had to come down but not by the way I constructed it, piece by piece, but with a full-blown blast. I was married with a loving family and well on my way to completing a duel Masters Degree program. I was considered somewhat intelligent, but I knew the truth about what was going on inside of me. I wanted out of this closet. I had faith in God and believe it or not, for years I went along never thinking about this closet or the brick wall I had erected. I stayed busy,

busy, and so busy that when the thoughts would come to remind me of what and whom I needed to deal with, I would take on another project and bury myself deeper in the closet.

Two things happened that provided me with the strength I needed to open this closet door and begin to blast a hole in this gigantic wall I had lived and surrounded myself with. Remember when I spoke earlier of how two powerful resources, knowledge and information, can change any situation or people if they were applied correctly? Well, I discovered two significant pieces of information that helped change the course of my life.

The first was a powerful scripture tucked away in the King James Bible in the Book of Psalms, Chapter 139:13-14. It reads: For You formed my inward parts; You covered me in my mother's womb. I will praise You, for I am fearfully and wonderfully made. Marvelous are Your works, and that my soul knows very well. I began to confess this scripture every single day of my life. Wherever I went and whomever would talk to me heard this scripture. It literally changed the way I saw myself. My worn and wrinkled hangs began to change their position. I could now lift them up regardless of who was watching. I knew without reservations and misgivings that I was on my way. I could finally reach back and provide some sort of strength for my siblings who faced their own tumultuous bouts. We were a set of nine separated, dysfunctional and lonely sisters and brothers with questions for Jesus about His love and protection for us during the many years we spent as wards of the State of Indiana.

My mother had always insisted we develop our relationships with Jesus. A strong Christian foundation was important to her. My mom knew long before the medical doctors that we would not have her with us throughout our teenage and adult lives. She started early with talks, Bible readings and stories of how we needed each other and if at all possible, we were never to lose contact with one another even though we had been split into five different foster homes from Indiana to Missouri. The last evening we all saw my mom alive as a family was at a tuberculosis center on October 7, 1965. We can all remember her final talks about Jesus and His love for her. She sent us to church when she herself was physically unable to go. She informed us that we could always call on Jesus and He would take care of us. Now, all we wanted Jesus to do was provide us with answers and tell us the purpose of this turbulent journey we had taken. We all needed to come out of closets that held us captive, but we didn't know how without succumbing to more damage. It finally needed to be said.

Truth can be detrimental but necessary. The folks that abused us were the same deep, chocolate hues as us; they were my own people. They enjoyed the fruits of financial gain that were provided to them by the State of Indiana that were supposed to be for our basic needs. Finally, we could at last talk about the treatment many of us endured. We didn't have an Oprah or Dr. Phil. There was no stage for us to sit on and express what our parents didn't do right. We simply had each other. We began to talk about what had transpired in each of our lives. It didn't matter that a foolish adult put a gun to my sisters head as a joke. It didn't t matter that my younger brother lost his right eye the very first day he was placed in the foster home at age eleven, or that one of my sisters had her hair cut and hands scalded. Two of my brothers were locked in a room in the basement of a luxury home of a minister while the family left for a weekend excursion. The authorities removed them when neighbors informed them that they didn't see my brothers in the automobile as it was departing. It didn't matter that another sister and I had to use our hands to cover our private areas as we slept. We used them (our hands) as front doors were open for us at night when we would return home from different places. They were shields from dirty, old hands trying to feel on them. Our hands were never lifted, but dropped to provide protection. But for me, it didn't matter anymore about those men who called me names for not sleeping with them and then enjoyed laughing at me about it.

It no longer mattered that I had used these hands to clean toilets to help pay for my college education. It didn't matter that on occasions, I along with my sisters and brothers, had gone to bed hungry. It didn't matter about the sugar sandwiches we had taken to school for lunch. It didn't matter that I had burned up a pair of socks in the oven attempting to dry them before going to school. It didn't even matter that at one time we all had to share the same bath water from a large Number Two tub. It didn't matter anymore that the State of Indiana had reversed their decision and returned some of my sisters and brothers back to my dad, only to be taken again and placed back into the system. It didn't matter anymore that I had questions about my own sexuality. I thought for sure I was messed up, unfit to be loved because of my past. It didn't matter that I had spent the summer of 1961 in the hospital with some disease called Lockjaw, paralyzed from the waist down. I had cut my right elbow on a piece of rusted tin and hadn't received the tetanus shots prior to, but thanks be to God for His mercies. I knew I was fearfully and wonderfully made and none of it mattered anymore. I had found the courage to tell the truth about the mayhem and all its ugliness it had created in my life. I was going to make it.

One by one the bricks were coming down. I wanted a full-blown implosion, but there was something else I needed to face. I needed to face the one person still alive who had taken advantage of my personal temple. I needed to hear myself set him free. When I was granted the opportunity to see him, I looked him dead in his face and I asked him to forgive me for the bitterness I had carried around. I wanted to release him and myself. He never said one word, but I was free. I had confessed on the inside of me and I could feel the BLAST taking place. I remember walking away vowing never, never, never ever to blame myself again. I knew without any uncertainty that I could open the closet door wider and wider. My hands were released so I could lift them up to praise God. There is much more I could share with you regarding my siblings but it's important that you know they are all free now and doing well. They, like me, have found the strength they needed to open the closet door and most of their worn and wrinkled hands are lifted up. I know our mother and father are smiling on us from above. We are free.

The second piece of information that served as a turning point to help change my self perception came from information I received about my maternal great-grand father in 1984 at a family reunion. Thank God for technology and the ability we have to research news. When the Civil War ended in 1865, I now know that my maternal great-grand father was a runaway slave and later a free man who resided with his family in the state of Mississippi. I was provided with documented evidence that verified that several years later, and after his escape from slavery, that freedom was still not a total reality for most blacks. One night while my great-grand father was still a teenager, he slipped away and swam to his freedom across the Mississippi River to the state of Arkansas. Upon his arrival in Arkansas, he felt it necessary to change his name. This historical and trailblazing defiance gave me a new surge of courage to continue my release from the years of bondage I had suffered. If my great-grand father could survive the journey he undertook, then why couldn't I? I'm sure if he could share with me the purpose and plans God had for his destiny he would. I have told the truth in spite of my worn and wrinkled hands. I am a thankful granny who chooses every single day to come out of the closet.

I take a deep breath each morning I am allowed to wake up. I'm reminded of how God created me in His image and likeness and as long as I can show up, I confess I will be a proactive, productive 55 year-old granny with things to do and places to go. I want to be remembered by all my grandchildren as a granny who told the truth in spite of her wrinkled and worn old hands. My prayer for all grannies would be that if you had to use your hands for protection against someone who violated you, find your connection with the Lord Jesus Christ. In your relationship with Him, he will provide you with the strength to overcome any pain you may have suffered.

Only Jesus can help you change the overwhelming circumstances that may have taken place in your life and how you see yourself. Jesus Christ will provide you the opportunity to come out of your closet and tell the truth, and then it's up to you to grab the scriptures and hear yourself declare that you are fearfully and wonderfully made in His Image. Use the information and the knowledge Jesus Christ gives you about His love for you. Do a study in the Scriptures and find out the plans He has always had concerning you. You may have come from a dysfunctional family or maybe you were separated like my family was, but please let the Lord Jesus Christ provide you with the extreme makeover you need. You will never be the same! I guarantee it.

Chapter 8

Granny's Hands Assumes the Position

One of the Laws of the Land

I would like to think by now that my grandson can understand why granny's hands are old. He has spent the last several years of his life living in Michigan interacting with me on a weekly basis. He has encountered other grannies from church, the library and other social events we have attended. I would hope through his eyes he might see and understand that like his own granny, most grannies hands may look old but they have stories and journeys to share. Like his me, most of these grannies have learned to assume the position on behalf of their sons and daughters and grandchildren.

Remember Michael, my own son who took the road trip with me at the beginning when I started this awesome journey of sharing where my hands had been? I didn't reveal too much about him except that he was the only one brave enough to trust me traveling to Jacksonville, North Carolina, to be a source of comfort to his older sister as we waited for the arrival of my first grandson. Oh yeah, he was only eleven so he had no choice.

Michael also entered our lives in the month of March; the same cold, bitter and sometimes rough month when I lost both my parents. March is also the month where people have to reorganize their lives, pay bills from the past Christmas season and handle whatever else looms over their heads. My Michael arrived as a bundle of joy that changed our lives yet again.

I must share with you how there came to be a baby boy named Michael. Michael's dad is one of nineteen siblings straight from the South. His family is loaded with sons, uncles and male children. He wanted me to assign initials (M.D.) to Michael's name, instead of a full name. His grandfather was named R.D., one of his uncles was named C.B., and there was an uncle T.J. Well, can you imagine after nine moths of carrying this precious child inside of me that surely he had to be given a full-fledged name. I wanted something with character and integrity. I knew the Biblical account regarding the warrior angel Michael who had to be dispatched to help render the answer to the prophet Daniel after he had sought God in prayer concerning his people (Daniel, Chapter 10 NIV Bible). Until the archangel Michael showed up, Daniel had been waiting for an answer after fasting twenty-one days. I have told my son all his life that when he shows up changes must be made, positive changes.

I have instructed Michael diligently about the importance of his name and the responsibilities associated with it. I am not foolish enough to believe that he's has been an angel. That would be a lie but he has been told and just a few years ago, he made a decision and demonstrated to us the lessons we had taught him were being received. Michael decided to step up and provide blood for his niece that was born prematurely in Memphis. He and I made a trip to the local blood bank and gave blood. My granddaughter arrived at 1 pound, 8 ounces and she is alive and well today five years later. He has the makings of a great man and his family is very proud of those actions.

My son has been told from day one the position he must assume if he plans on making a difference in this world we live in. He's been taught the importance of respect, character, and most importantly his role as an African-American male living in the United States. Michael's been educated about the Lord Jesus Christ and Martin Luther King Jr., Nelson Mandela, Rodney King, Fredrick Douglas, Marcus Garvey, William Tucker, Cornel West and Jasper, Texas. He is aware of his own father's struggles as a man of color living within the boundaries of a racist world. He understands that many of those boundaries that were placed around him for him were there because his father desired to give him a life that would afford him the opportunity to live as freely as possible from all signs of racism and the social and economic injustices imposed on people of color. Michael recognizes how hard his father has worked to feed and clothe him. My son has heard the sermons from him pleading with him to complete his education, make good choices when away from home, show up on time for work, save some money, buy some land and leave something as a legacy and if all else fails in his world, God will wait for him to enter His. He has no excuse! Dress rehearsal is over!

Michael always been aware of his past, acquainted with his present and very hopeful about his future. He realizes the importance of wearing a belt and the consequences for dropping his pants before marriage. My husband and I will walk him through the court system to carry out his duties of early fatherhood if he should surrender to foolishness. With all that said, I have instructed Michael about the position to assume if he is ever stopped by any type of law enforcement anywhere within or outside this great nation. He stands exactly 6 feet, 2 inches tall, 272 pounds and he's been blessed to have one of the darkest shades of chocolate skin tones. It's as if the bright glow from the sun and the moon came together in a magical conversation to etch this color just for him. His eyes invite you inside to have brief talks about the stories he's been told all his life and yes, there's such a sweetness and gentle spirit that follows him. I had no choice but to teach, train and capture his attention. I know his journey will take him before great men. I also realize the price he must pay for traveling on such a treacherous road. I had no choice.

Many of you as may feel the restrictions placed on my son were uncalled for, some may even surmise that we have put too much pressure on him and the parameters are unrealistic, but Michael is cognizant of assuming the position of lifting his hands up and surrendering. Surrendering not because he's being cocky or smart, but mindful that we would rather have him alive than beat to death and brain dead, unable to make decisions about his own basic needs. He is heedful of that language of respect to exercise if stopped by law enforcement. He is careful not to break and run because if he does, he may not be able to but we can vividly conjure up and replay all those gruesome pictures of all those young, black males from the past and present who failed to assume the position. They now lay in the cemetery with their dreams silently resting in the cold, clammy dust and dirt that covers the shell of their bodies that once housed all their potential futures. My son already understands but most importantly, he knows his mother also assumes another position on his behalf. My old hands are also extended in an uplifted position, not because I have been stopped by law enforcement but because I know that when I raise my old hands up, I am demonstrating to the Lord Jesus Christ the honor and respect due Him. I am evoking His presence in my life, while giving Him permission to lead and guide me as I offer Michael back to him.

Just as my grandson's comments got my attention, my uplifted hands get God's. Like the grannies across this nation that spend time looking at their old hands, their little ones have no idea of what's involved in raising them. I challenge every son and grandson to make the effort to talk to their granny about her old hands. I challenge you to ask her for the wisdom and instruction that were passed on to her from the Book of Proverbs that instructs her to lead and guide her sons. Telling them the stories left as an example for them from the word of God..

I look at my old hands each and every day; the wrinkles are real and the signs of aging have caught up with me. Most times my hands are in need of a manicure or nail polish. I keep a coat of plain old petroleum jelly on them, lessons learned from the old school. They're my hands! I thank God for them. I realize that one day I too will pass to the other side but my hands have held me in times of sorrow, times of trusting the Lord, times of wiping the tears from my weary eyes but most of all, it's been in those times of lifting them up that I've found peace.

Every journey I've encountered and every time I've elevated my hands, sometimes with the tears meeting underneath my cheeks, I keep them uplifted. Up because I have sons and grandsons, nephews and still some uncles that need this granny with old hands to intercede on their behalf. To God be the glory. I challenge grannies everywhere to become radical with new missions of loving yourselves first then others. Do something special for yourselves and with yourself. Begin to see the beauty in your hands. Regardless of where you've taken your hands, it's never too late to raise them to the Lord Jesus Christ. Remember, "you are truly, fearfully and wonderfully created in the image of God." Let's lift our old hands up. I now realize just how valuable my life is to those I have been entrusted to love and care for.

I also realize that in order for me to continue my journey I have to take responsibility and ownership for the time I am allowed to live on this earth. I desire to make a difference and if this work can serve as a new beginning for those who have read it, then any shame and humiliation I may feel by sharing some of my experiences or from the harsh words from those trained critics that may take pleasure in ripping apart this book, will not have been in vain.

Assume the position; it's the law of God's and His decree for all of us to lift our old hands. To all the young men, women and boys and girls, God has provided all the information we will ever need to help change our great nation. Once we learn to utilize the technology we have and implore the God-given knowledge stored in all of us, the position of praising and worshiping God will set us all free. I know, I did it. I assume the position each and every day!

About the Author

Celestine Starks resides in Lansing, Michigan with her husband, Preston Starks. She has been bless to have five wonderful adult children and twelve grandchildren. She has always served in her local community in some capacity for the past twenty-five plus years. She is employed by Michigan State University was she works as a Community Development Specialist with interests in Distress Communities and Public Housing Residents. She loves people and desires the same opportunities to be available to all and any person brave enough to ask God for the strength and courage to come out of their closet. She has written and produced several plays shown at local churches and throughout the Lansing area. Her greatest accomplishment has been the relationship she has with the Lord Jesus Christ. She has been a member of the New Jerusalem Church for thirty-one years where she serves faithfully as an usher.

Printed in the United States
45032LVS00001B/205-225